Your
Prayerful
JOURNAL
for Advent

Bridget Mary Meehan

LIGUORI
PUBLICATIONS

One Liguori Drive
Liguori, MO 63057-9999
(314) 464-2500

Imprimi Potest:
James Shea, C.SS.R.
Provincial, St. Louis Province
The Redemptorists

Imprimatur:
Monsignor Maurice F. Byrne
Vice Chancellor, Archdiocese of St. Louis

ISBN 0-89243-524-0
Library of Congress Catalog Card Number: 93-78435

Copyright © 1993, Liguori Publications
Printed in the United States of America

All rights reserved. No part of this book may be reproduced, stored in a
retrieval system, or transmitted without the written permission of Liguori
Publications.

Scripture quotations are taken from THE NEW AMERICAN BIBLE WITH
REVISED NEW TESTAMENT, copyright © 1986, AND THE REVISED PSALMS,
copyright © 1991, by the Confraternity of Christian Doctrine, Wash-
ington, D.C., and are used with permission. All rights reserved.

Excerpts from the English translation of *Lectionary for Mass*, copyright ©
1969, International Committee on English in the Liturgy, Inc. (ICEL);
excerpts from the English translation of *The Roman Missal*, copyright ©
1973, ICEL, are used with permission. All rights reserved.

Art and design by Andy Willman

This book is dedicated to my family,
who taught me so much
about the spiritual journey
by their joyful faith, prayerful spirit,
and Christian witness:
Mom and Dad,
Aunt Molly,
Patrick and Val,
Sean and Nancy,
my niece, Katie,
and my nephew, Danny.

Contents

Acknowledgments

In writing this book, I am grateful to my family and friends. The gift of their faith and friendship is a constant source of strength. I am especially thankful to my parents, Bridie and Jack Meehan, who taught me so much about God's love by their love for me. I am also grateful to my Aunt Molly McCarthy and to my brothers and sisters-in-law, Sean and Nancy, Patrick and Valerie, my niece, Katie, and my nephew, Danny. Their goodness and kindness bring constant joy.

I owe a special debt of gratitude to the following Sisters in my religious community, the Society of Sisters for the Church, who have encouraged me along the way: Regina Madonna Oliver, Mary Emma Hadrick, Melanie Maczka. I am grateful for the prayer support of all the members of the society.

I thank my friends from the Fort Myer Chapel community who have encouraged me through the years: Irene Marshall, Peg and Bob Bowen, Francis L. Keefe, Donna Mogan, Joseph Mulqueen, Ana Minassian, Wayne Schmid, Bob Schaaf, Sandra Voelker, John Weyand, Carol and Ray Buchanan, Walter Montondon, Bruce and Yolando Burslie, Marie and Steve Billick, Mike Pollitt, Jim Jones, Daisy Sullivan, Millie Nash, Larry Skummer, Ron Whalen, Elizabeth Hosington, Mary and Dick Guertin, Doris Mason, Maria Kemp, Debbie Dubuque, Fritz and Barbara Warren, Peter Julianne, Charlotte Reynierse, Michael Morsche, Mark Evans, Kenny Connors, Marie and Bill Dillon, Helen Groff, Bennie Rossler, Anita Eggert, Tony and Ottie Nadora, Phil and Diane Pons, Bob and Sharon Schoeffner, Ken Schroeder, Monika Etsell, Patricia Herlihy, Jack Klingenhagen, Mike Marshall, Charles McDonnell, Mary Cashmen, Roseanne Fedorko, Doc Wempe, Denis and Sue Wenzel, and Phil Stewart.

Introduction

Advent is a season of joyful hope and spiritual expectation. The prophet Isaiah invites us to wait in patient hope and to live with the stresses and uncertainties of contemporary life, trusting that God is faithful.

"Prepare the way of the Lord" (Luke 3:4). The prophetic cry of John the Baptist reminds us that *now* is the time to prepare for the coming of the Lord. The Lord is close to us—now. God comes into our lives and into our world to save us from sin—now, to set us free from bondage—now, to liberate us from anxiety—now, and to love us into fullness of life—now. God comes to satisfy the longing of our hearts for peace, joy, and justice. The reign of God is in our midst—now.

God Dwelling Among Us

But how can this be? In a world where violence, rape, drug addiction, hostility, injustice, hatred, abuse, theft, discrimination, and countless other indignities abound, how can God be present? In our own lives, when we experience emptiness, stress, doubt, inner turmoil, anxiety, loss, fear, and depression, we wonder if God really cares about us.

The good news is that Jesus became human to show the depths of God's love for us in our sinfulness, guilt, weakness, and pain. Jesus enters into our humanity to bring us salvation, healing, and joy. Jesus, Emmanuel, the compassion of God dwelling among us, is always loving us with infinite, passionate, forgiving, healing, love.

Nothing, not even the Christmas rush, should disturb our peace. Christmas shopping, card writing, tree decorating, food preparation, and holiday parties need not overwhelm us. They can, in fact, become an important part of our spiritual preparation for Christ's coming. We can bring all these activities into the presence of God, knowing that

God will transform us. We can trust that God's glory will shine forth in everything we do to prepare for Christmas. God will save us from all that could separate us from God and from one another:

> "Behold our God, to whom we looked to save us!...
> let us rejoice and be glad that he has saved us!"
> Isaiah 25:9

Welcoming Jesus

During this Advent season, we take time to pray, to still our anxious hearts, to open ourselves to the God who calls us by name and speaks to us in the ordinary events and relationships of our lives. We take time to journey to the center of our being, to reflect on the mystery of Christ's coming into our world. There, in the center of our being, we are challenged to let go of our preoccupations and worries, to trust that God will take infinitely better care of us, our loved ones, and our world than we could ever imagine. All we have to do is invite God to come and love us in our neediness and emptiness. Throughout Advent, we pray, "Come, Lord Jesus, set us free, heal us, transform us, empower us."

This Advent, experience God's boundless love by using your imagination in prayer. For example, during prayer imagine that you meet Jesus in a Scripture story. Using your imagination you may *see* Jesus, *hear* him, or *sense* his presence. You may simply *know* Jesus through abstract thought or reason. Perhaps your experience of Jesus through your imagination will be a combination of these.

You may realize the presence of God dwelling in all creation in the experience of silence. As you choose to say and do nothing, *be* in love with God; become one with God in the embrace of silence.

There is no correct or incorrect way to pray. The maxim is simply be open to the graced intuitions that God reveals to you in prayer—and follow them. In other words, pray as you can, not as you can't.

Your Advent Journey

Your Prayerful Journal for Advent offers an opportunity to journey through Advent with a greater sense of God's nearness, to discover God's presence everywhere, and to wait for a deeper coming of Christ in daily life and in all creation. It is an opportunity to become more responsive to God through prayerful reflection.

Each week of Advent has a theme. Week One is Waiting in Hope, Week Two is Preparing in Love, Week Three is Rejoicing in Christ, Week Four is Praying the O Antiphons. Developing the theme each week is a simple prayer plan combining a brief Scripture passage, meditation, or prayer, with thought-provoking questions for reflection and a prayer exercise. Because the images, feelings, and insights that emerge during prayer reflect the unique persons we are and play an important role in our spiritual development, space is provided for personal thoughts, feelings, insights, images—in other words—the inner movements of the Spirit.

Individuals, members of small faith-sharing groups, Bible-study participants, RCIA candidates, sponsors, lay-ministry groups, and pastoral teams will find *Your Prayerful Journal for Advent* a helpful resource for spiritual growth during the Advent season.

Week One
Waiting in Hope

Introduction

Waiting is difficult; we don't like to wait; we want instant results. Notice how advertisements promise everything from quick weight loss to a comprehensive knowledge of computers in just four weeks.

The same kind of "instant result" orientation can affect our spiritual life. We try one retreat after another, read as many spiritual books as possible, attend as many self-help programs as we can fit into our hectic schedules—all in an attempt to become "more spiritual," "holier," or a "better pastoral leader." So often we experience frustration and disappointment when we don't see immediate results or when our efforts fail. There is another way.

During the Advent season, we listen to the advice of the prophet Isaiah challenging us to wait patiently. God will not forget us. God is with us in all our struggles. God does not expect instant results in us but waits patiently and lovingly as we struggle with our weaknesses and inabilities to reach many of the goals we so feverishly set for ourselves. God looks into our hearts and appreciates the gradual unfolding of beauty, love, and goodness within us. God patiently continues to heal what is broken, damaged, or hurt within us. God continues to give us the greatest gift of all: the gift of God's self. God, indeed, fulfills the deepest desires of our hearts by loving us unconditionally. All we need do is wait in hope.

How do you wait in hope? You wait in hope through prayer. Take time each day for quiet and solitude, to be attentive to the God who dwells within you. Let go of all preconceptions and fears. Be open and listen to God. *Be* in love with God and contemplate God's presence and power in every aspect of your life, in your relationships, in your work or ministry, and in the wonders of creation.

Week One, Day One

On that day,
The branch of the LORD
will be luster and glory,
and the fruit of the earth
will be honor and splendor
for the survivors of Israel....
For over all, his glory
will be shelter and protection:
shade from the parching
heat of day,
refuge and cover
from storm and rain.

Isaiah 4:2, 6

Reflections

In this Scripture passage, Isaiah tells us that God will never abandon us or fail to protect us. Recall an important experience in your life that helped you trust God. In what ways have you grown spiritually because of this experience?

Where are you being called to grow in trust at the present time? How is God calling you to foster this growth?

How are you resisting this growth?

What gifts and insights do you find in yourself that help you wait in hope for God?

Waiting in Hope

1. Relax. Close your eyes. Take several deep breaths.

2. Read the Scripture verse slowly and thoughtfully.

3. In a prayerful conversation with God, share your responses to the previous reflections. Listen to what God may wish to share with you. (You may wish to record key insights from this conversation in a prayer journal for further reflection.)

4. Spend time in silence, waiting in hope and *being* in love with God.

5. God dwells within you and speaks to you all the time, not in an audible way but through an inner voice in the depths of your heart. You are in a constant loving communion with God, who chooses you as a favorite dwelling place. Reflect on the impact that God dwelling within you has on your life.

6. During this time of prayer, ask God to reveal to you how much you are loved.

7. Be aware of any thoughts, feelings, images, or insights that emerge during your prayer time. Share these with God. (Record these, if you wish, in your prayer journal.)

Week One, Day Two

As the deer longs
for streams of water,
so my soul longs for you,
O God.
My being thirsts for God,
the living God.
When can I go and see
the face of God?

Psalms 42–43:2-3

Reflections

In what ways have you experienced a yearning for God?

What obstacles do you need to overcome to experience a deeper communion with God?

How have you helped others experience a deeper desire for God?

How can you become more receptive to the God you long to love more deeply?

Waiting in Hope

1. Following a few minutes of silence, focus on the yearning for God you experience in the depths of your being.

2. Allow that yearning to pray within you.

3. Be aware of any thoughts, feelings, or images that occur.

4. Become aware of God's yearning for you.

5. Relax in silence and allow God to love you. Allow yourself to receive whatever God most desires to give you.

6. As an expression of your longing for God, slowly recite the following psalm. You may wish to do so using the suggestions above.

> *O God, you are my God—*
> *for you I long!*
> *For you my body yearns;*
> *for you my soul thirsts,*
> *Like a land parched, lifeless,*
> *and without water.*
> *So I look to you in the sanctuary*
> *to see your power and glory.*
> *For your love is better than life;*
> *my lips offer you worship!*
> *I will bless you as long as I live;*
> *I will lift up my hands, calling on your name.*
> *My soul shall savor the rich banquet of praise,*
> *with joyous lips my mouth shall honor you!*
> Psalm 63:2-6

7. Be aware of any thoughts, emotions, images, or insights that occur during your prayer experience. (Record these, if you wish, in your prayer journal.)

Week One, Day Three

But a shoot shall sprout
from the stump of Jesse,
and from his roots
a bud shall blossom.
The spirit of the LORD
shall rest upon him:
a spirit of wisdom
and of understanding,
A spirit of counsel and of strength,
a spirit of knowledge
and of fear of the LORD.

Isaiah 11:1-2

Reflections

In this Scripture passage, Isaiah tells us that God sends the Spirit into our hearts with the gifts of wisdom, counsel, strength, knowledge, and fear of the Lord and that we are to wait in hope for such a time of the Spirit. Recall an important experience in your life when you waited in hope for the Spirit's coming. Be aware of any thoughts, feelings, images, or sensations that may come to you. How can you open yourself to the fullness of the Spirit's presence in your life now?

What are the major obstacles that keep you from waiting in hope for the Spirit's coming in your life now?

How have you helped others to be more receptive to the Spirit's gifts in their lives?

What can you do to share the gifts of the Spirit with others?

Waiting in Hope

(Soft instrumental music may provide a beautiful background for this prayer experience.)

1. Relax your mind and body.

2. Focus on your breathing. As you breathe in, imagine the Spirit of God filling you with whatever gifts you need at this time in your life.

3. As you breathe out, imagine the Spirit of God flowing through you and out to others to gift them with God's love.

4. Be aware of how the Spirit has gifted you and others. Be open to new ways the Spirit may be calling you to wait in hope.

5. Consider how the Spirit is calling you to new possibilities of service and ministry in the Church. Consider your Spirit-given gifts that will enable you to respond. Read and reflect on the gifts listed in 1 Corinthians 12:4-11 (wisdom, knowledge, faith, healing, mighty deeds, prophecy, discernment of spirits, varieties of tongues, interpretation of tongues).

6. Pray for the grace to wait in hope for those gifts the Spirit may wish to give you to build up the Body of Christ.

7. In a loving conversation with God, share any thoughts, feelings, images, or insights you become conscious of during your prayer time. (Record these, if you wish, in your prayer journal.)

Week One, Day Four

*For creation awaits with eager
expectation the revelation of the
children of God....We know that all
creation is groaning in labor pains even
until now; and not only that, but we
ourselves, who have the firstfruits of the
Spirit, we also groan within ourselves as
we wait for adoption, the redemption of
our bodies. For in hope we were saved.*

*Now hope that sees for itself is not
hope. For who hopes for what one sees?
But if we hope for what we do not see,
we wait with endurance.*

Romans 8:19, 22-25

Reflections

Saint Paul describes creation and humanity as experiencing the suffering of labor and childbirth in the following images: "groaning in labor pains" (v. 22) and waiting with "eager expectation" (v. 19) and with "endurance" (v. 25). In what ways can the process of labor and childbirth help you understand how to wait with hope for new birth in your spiritual life?

In what ways do you think creation is experiencing a new birth today?

Do you find Paul's image of God as the Birther of New Life helpful in understanding the process of spiritual growth? If so, why? If not, why not?

How can you help others experience new birth in their spiritual lives this Advent?

Waiting in Hope

1. Breathe deeply, slowly, and rhythmically through your nose so that the abdomen rises as you breathe in and lowers as you breathe out through your mouth. Spend a few minutes doing this deep-breathing exercise.

2. Imagine God, the Birther of New Life, waiting to give birth to you, spiritually and emotionally, with "eager expectation" (v. 19), "groaning in labor pains" (v. 22), filled with "hope" (v. 24) and with patient "endurance" (v. 25).

3. As you reflect on God, who is like a mother giving birth to you, become aware of any images, feelings, sensations, or memories.

4. Imagine God waiting to give birth to all creation, to all human life, to the entire cosmo with "eager expectation" (v. 19), "groaning in labor pains" (v. 22), filled with "hope" (v. 24) and with "endurance" (v. 25). Use all your senses to experience God giving birth to all of life.

5. As you reflect on God, the mother giving birth to all of life, become aware of any insights, images, feelings, sensations, or memories you experience.

6. Reflect upon any experience you've had of bringing forth new life (physical birth, painting a picture, designing a new program, writing a poem). Consider what you have learned from this experience about waiting in hope for God's coming. Consider how this experience enriched your spiritual growth.

7. Be aware of any feelings, thoughts, insights, or images that occur during this prayer time. (Record these, if you wish, in your prayer journal.)

Week One, Day Five

Lord our God,
with the birth of your Son,
your glory breaks on the world.
Through the night hours
of the darkened earth
we your people watch
for the coming
of your promised Son.
As we wait, give us a foretaste
of the joy that you will grant us
when the fullness of his glory
has filled the earth,
who lives and reigns with you
for ever and ever.

Alternate Opening Prayer for
Christmas Mass at Midnight

Reflections

What recent experience has taught you to wait until God strengthens you and frees you from fear and anxiety?

How can you learn to wait well for the fulfillment of your longing for God?

How has prayer and meditation helped you wait for God to act in your life?

How can you be more patient with people in your life who are anxious and afraid?

Waiting in Hope

1. Become completely still. Relax and breathe deeply.

2. Reflect on the meaning of the Opening Prayer for Christmas Mass at Midnight.

3. Ask God to reveal the fears and anxieties that keep you from opening yourself more deeply to God.

4. Through the day, be attentive to the ways God's glory breaks into your life. Be aware of the difference this consciousness makes in your day's events.

5. Know that God's love surrounds you. Rediscover your longing for God in the ordinary experiences of life, such as waiting for the traffic light to change, the baby to fall asleep, a friend to call. Every event, person, and situation can become an opportunity to encounter God and deepen your yearning for God's presence in your life.

6. Become aware of anything you feel called to do as a result of your prayerful reflection on your experiences of waiting.

7. In a prayerful conversation with God, share any insights, feelings, or thoughts that emerge. Record any important insights from this conversation in your prayer journal. These writings make for rich further reflection.

Week One, Day Six

The Lord GOD will wipe away
the tears from all faces;
The reproach of his people
he will remove
from the whole earth;
for the LORD has spoken.
On that day it will be said:
"Behold our God,
to whom we looked to save us!
This is the LORD
for whom we looked;
let us rejoice and be glad
that he has saved us!"

Isaiah 25:8-9

Reflections

God will satisfy the desires of your heart for healing and consolation. How are you presently involved in bringing God's healing and comfort to others?

How can Christians be a sign of divine compassion to the world?

What is God revealing to you about waiting in hope in this Scripture passage? What impact might this have on your ability to console and comfort others?

What simple thing can you do today to be an instrument of God's peace in your family? at work? in the Church? in your neighborhood? nation? world?

Waiting in Hope

1. Relax your body by letting go of any stress you feel in your muscles. Move from the top of your head to the bottom of your feet, alternately releasing and tightening the muscles in each area of your body. Stand up and stretch your arms upward, counting to ten.

2. Call on God to comfort and heal you. Recall the promise of verse nine in Isaiah 25: "...let us rejoice and be glad that he has saved us!"

3. Pray for the gift of a compassionate heart so that God's comfort and healing love can flow through you to others.

4. In openness to the healing love of God in your life and in the world, pray the following prayer for those who are experiencing alienation, division, hostility, and misunderstanding:

Lord, make me an instrument of your peace,
where there is hatred, let me sow love,
where there is injury, pardon,
where there is doubt, faith,
where there is despair, hope,
where there is darkness, light,
and where there is sadness, joy,

O divine Master, grant that I may not so much
seek to be consoled as to console,
to be understood as to understand,
to be loved as to love.

For it is in giving that we receive;
it is in pardoning that we are pardoned;
and it is in dying that we are born into eternal life.

Daily Readings With
Saint Francis Assisi

5. Imagine God touching with consolation and healing each person or group you are praying for. Be aware of any thoughts, images, feelings, or insights that emerge. (Record these, if you wish, in your prayer journal.)

6. Recall a time when you encouraged someone who was depressed or lonely. Ask God for the strength to be a channel of God's healing, compassionate love for the people who need you the most.

7. Decide on one thing you will do to be an instrument of God's peace—today.

Week One, Day Seven

*Yet the LORD is waiting
to show you favor,
and he rises to pity you;
For the LORD is a God of justice:
blessed are all who wait for him!*

Isaiah 30:18

Reflections

In what ways have you experienced God's favor and justice in your life?

In what ways have you worked to free the oppressed and to make the world a more loving and just place?

How have you helped others face major crises in their lives?

Can you make a phone call, write a letter, donate money, or do something concrete to help the needy and oppressed members of society?

Waiting in Hope

1. Begin your prayer by relaxing and breathing deeply. Imagine that you are in an elevator descending slowly from the twentieth floor. Close your eyes and count as you slowly descend:
   "20...19...18...16...14...11...7...4...2...1..."

2. Now, slowly read the Scripture verse again. Reflect on its meaning in your life. Reflect on the impact this Scripture verse can have on the lives of the poor and oppressed members of society.

3. Pray for victims of oppression and discrimination: for the poor, jobless, homeless, and refugees. Ask God to help you identify ways to minister to their needs.

4. As you pray today, be aware that God is loving those for whom you are praying. You may wish to pray for anyone in need or groups of people who are suffering from injustice and oppression. Allow the Spirit to lead you. As you pray, imagine God liberating, healing, and empowering each person and group.

5. Observe how God embraces each person who is oppressed with liberating, healing love, and removes all pain, hurt, anger, disappointment, and injustice.

6. Pray for the oppressors of God's people. Observe how God turns to the oppressors who are waiting for forgiveness and embraces them with healing love. Observe how God calls all people to live together in justice and peace according to the values of the gospel.

7. Pray the Lord's Prayer for all those who wait for liberation from injustice. Pray that they may experience the God who loves them and waits with them to strengthen them in their efforts. Ask God to reveal to you how you can express your solidarity with the oppressed and work for a more just world.

Week Two
Preparing in Love

Introduction

Advent is a time to make ready our hearts for Christ's coming. Preparing our hearts in love for the coming of Christ, of course, does not happen in four weeks. It is a lifetime journey of conversion, healing, and transformation. It is about creating a new heart and making space in our lives for the inbreaking of the holy.

Father Henri Nouwen offers some helpful insights on how to do this:

> Jesus asks us to shift the point of gravity, to relocate the center of our attention, to change our priorities to the "one necessary thing," to move our hearts to the center, where all other things fall into place....Jesus does not speak of a change of activities....He speaks of a change of heart. This makes everything different, even while everything appears to be the same.
> *Making All Things New*

When we begin to do this, we discover that all our concerns become gifts that deepen the new life we have found. Suffering, hurt, disappointment, loss, poverty, and anguish may continue to be part of our experience, but these very events become part and parcel of making our hearts ready to receive the Lord. They become moments when we are embraced by God. At these times, we can ask, "What in me needs to 'go deeper' to prepare in love for Christ's coming in my life?"

During this Advent season, we can choose to "go deeper," to open ourselves on a new level to conversion, healing, and transformation. We can journey in prayer to the center of our being where Jesus dwells. There we can experience the inbreaking of God's healing love in every area of our lives, creating within us a new heart. At this center, we can learn to prepare in love for Christ's coming every day of our lives.

Week Two, Day One

Comfort, give comfort to my people,
says your God.
Speak tenderly to Jerusalem,
and proclaim to her
that her service is at an end,
her guilt is expiated;
Indeed, she has received
from the hand of the LORD
double for all her sins.

Isaiah 40:1-2

Reflections

Have you experienced the tenderness of God? In what ways do you experience the comfort of God?

Is there some area in your life where you have lost heart? given up on yourself? given up on others? given up on God?

What is it that God desires to do in this situation to comfort you?

What can you do today to bring comfort to others? In what ways does bringing comfort to others prepare your heart for Christ's coming?

Preparing in Love

1. Breathe slowly and deeply.

2. Be aware that God's comforting love surrounds you. As you breathe in, imagine God's tender, gentle love flowing through you, comforting your family, friends, neighbors, and strangers.

3. Sometimes we lose heart in the desert of our loneliness, sinful behavior patterns, guilt, anxiety, fear, and broken relationships, like the Chosen People in this Scripture passage. At these times, we need God to lead us out of exile to our homeland. Be aware of any specific areas in your life that may need God's forgiveness and comfort. Ask God to tenderly embrace you in each of these areas.

4. Be open to whatever God wishes to do to comfort you and lead you out of exile to a deeper relationship with God and others.

5. In your verbal prayers, give thanks for rediscovering God's comforting, tender love in your personal desert.

6. Ask God to help you share this comforting love with those who are experiencing discouragement.

7. When you become aware of the sufferings of the poor and needy, pray Isaiah 40:1 for them: "Comfort, give comfort to my people."

Week Two, Day Two

For I am the LORD, *your God,*
who grasp your right hand;
It is I who say to you, "Fear not,
I will help you."

Isaiah 41:13

Reflections

Where do you experience anxiety and fear in your life? What are the sources of your fear and anxiety?

How does the image of God holding your hand in the midst of your anxiety and fear make you feel?

How does God's holding your hand affect the way you begin your activities this day?

What can you choose to do today that will reflect a deeper trust in God? How will this decision prepare your heart for Christ's coming?

Preparing in Love

1. Relax for a few moments in silence.

2. Recall a time in your life when you felt anxiety or fear. As you reflect on the situation, consider how God was present to you.

3. Imagine God holding your hand and delivering you from anxiety and fear in that particular situation.

4. Review your daily activities and relationships. Reflect on how God is holding your hand and delivering you from fear and anxiety now.

5. Express your gratitude to God for loving you so deeply during anxious times in your life, both present and past.

6. Ask God to help you grow in a deeper trust in God's loving presence in your life.

7. During the day, reflect upon this Scripture passage. Repeat these words as a calming mantra: "Fear not, I will help you" during times of fear and anxiety (Isaiah 41:13).

Week Two, Day Three

The afflicted and the needy seek
water in vain,
their tongues are parched
with thirst.
I, the LORD, will answer them;
I, the God of Israel,
will not forsake them.
I will open up rivers
on the bare heights,
and fountains in the broad valleys;
I will turn the desert
into a marshland,
and the dry ground into springs
of water.

Isaiah 41:17-18

Reflections

How do you witness to being a compassionate member of God's people?

In what ways have you given your time, energy, and resources to the poor and needy?

How is God calling you at the present time to minister to the needs of those who are suffering and in need among your family, friends, neighbors, strangers, the poor, and the homeless?

Why is this an important way to prepare your heart for Christ's coming?

Preparing in Love

1. Close your eyes. Become completely relaxed. Be still, centering yourself in God's compassionate heart.

2. Reflect on poverty, homelessness, and suffering. Pinpoint poverty and neediness in the lives of your family, friends, neighbors, and strangers in your community and in the world.

3. Be attentive to God's compassionate presence in the suffering of others.

4. Imagine God holding all the poor, needy, homeless, and broken people of the world in the divine heart of infinite compassion. Imagine fountains of living water flowing from God's heart, quenching their thirst with infinite love.

5. Give thanks for God's tenderness to the poor, the needy, and all those who suffer from any need.

6. Pray that you may become more sensitive to the suffering of the poor and needy in your family, neighborhood, local area, and in the world.

7. Decide on some practical act of service you can do to alleviate the suffering of others as a way of preparing your heart for Christ's coming this Christmas.

Week Two, Day Four

A voice cries out:
In the desert prepare the way
of the LORD!
Make straight in the wasteland
a highway for our God!
Every valley shall be filled in,
every mountain and hill
shall be made low;
The rugged land
shall be made a plain,
the rough country,
a broad valley.

Isaiah 40:3-4

Reflections

How are you preparing for Christ's coming?

What "valleys" need to be filled in your life? What "mountains" and "hills" need to be made low? What "paths" need to be straightened?

What obstacles keep you from making your heart ready for Christ's coming?

What is it that God desires to do in your life now to create a new heart within you?

Preparing in Love

1. Close your eyes. Become completely still. Be aware of your breathing. Feel the air as it moves in and out of your nostrils. Inhale and exhale slowly, allowing God's love to breathe in you.

2. Consider those areas in your life where you feel empty. Spend at least five minutes being still. With open hands and heart, pray that God's love will fill this emptiness in your life.

3. Invite God to redeem the obstacles in you that keep you from loving God and others. Spend another five minutes being still. With open hands and heart, pray that God's love will free you from these blockages and create within you a new heart.

4. Be attentive to any areas that need healing. Ask God to embrace you in each of these areas in your life and to love you tenderly and compassionately.

5. Consider what in you needs to "go deeper" to embrace God in your emptiness and brokenness.

6. Pray that God may fill the emptiness and remove the obstacles that block others (your family, friends, neighbors, the Church, society) from loving God and others.

7. Today, frequently repeat this brief portion of verse three from Isaiah 40: "...prepare the way of the LORD." Let it serve as a reminder that in everything you do or say, you are preparing your heart in love for the coming of Christ.

Week Two, Day Five

In those days John the Baptist
appeared, preaching in the desert of
Judea [and] saying, "Repent, for the
kingdom of heaven is at hand!"
It was of him that the prophet
Isaiah had spoken when he said:
"A voice of one crying out
in the desert,
'Prepare the way of the Lord,
make straight his paths.' "

"I am baptizing you with water,
for repentance, but the one who is
coming after me is mightier than I.
I am not worthy to carry his
sandals. He will baptize you with
the holy Spirit and fire."

Matthew 3:1-3,11

Reflections

Where do you experience the need for repentance in your life? What has been your greatest spiritual struggle? temptation? weakness?

During this Advent season, have you experienced the joy of God's forgiveness in the sacrament of reconciliation? If not, are you open to doing so? If not, why?

In what ways are you called to grow spiritually at the present time? How are you resisting this invitation to growth?

What can you do today to "let go and let God" help you overcome an area of sin or weakness in your life?

Preparing in Love

1. Be still. Breathe deeply. Relax your entire body. Imagine relaxation flowing through your body from head to toe. Focus on each area and imagine your body letting go of tension and becoming totally relaxed.

2. Reflect on the ministry of John the Baptist. Think about the major obstacles he encountered in preparing the people for the coming of the Lord.

3. We, like the people John preached to, are being called to journey out of the darkness of sin. We, too, need God to free us from the sins and weaknesses that keep us in bondage. Ask God to open your heart to the gift of God's forgiveness in your life. Ask God to open your heart to the grace of repentance. Consider those areas of your life where you need to experience forgiveness and repentance in order to prepare for Christ's coming this Advent.

4. Share with God your thoughts, feelings, fears, anxieties, or guilt about seeking forgiveness and repenting.

5. Invite God to free you of any obstacles or blockages that keep you from being receptive to God's mercy and from choosing to repent.

6. Decide on something specific you will do to experience God's forgiveness and demonstrate your repentance (celebrate the sacrament of reconciliation, forgive someone who has hurt you, ask forgiveness of someone you have offended, give generously of your time, energy, and money to the sick, the poor, or the needy).

7. Ask God to give you opportunities to share the liberating, healing power of God's forgiveness and the joy of repentance with others, especially those who are alienated from God and/or the Church.

Week Two, Day Six

We are on the way to you...

From the villages and towns,
from the hills and valleys,
with suffering brothers and sisters,
with laughing children.
as builders of peace,
as messengers of justice,
as witnesses to your love,
as members of your Church...

...we are on the way to you.

When we support the weak,
when we pray for the persecuted,
we are on the way to you.

When we celebrate your presence,
you are with your people.

A Latin American Hymn From
A Way to the Heart of Christmas
Brian Linard, Ed.

Reflections

In what ways are you preparing for the coming of Jesus by helping others?

How have you worked for peace and justice in your community? in the Church? nation? world?

Have you been generous with your resources toward those in need? How? If not, why?

Have you worked in partnership with others in Church and society to raise consciousness about and take a stance on social justice issues (respect for life, healthcare, hunger, spouse abuse, child abuse, housing, unemployment, racial discrimination, sexual discrimination, human rights violations, outreach to Third World countries, and care of the environment)?

Preparing in Love

1. Relax for a few moments and become centered.

2. Recall a time when you became especially conscious of
   Christ's presence in any of the following: your
   "suffering brothers and sisters," "laughing children,"
   "builders of peace," "messengers of justice," "witnesses"
   to God's love, "members" of the Church, "the weak"
   and "persecuted." Reflect about your experience and
   how life changed as a result of this experience.

3. Be aware of any thoughts, images, feelings, and insights
   that emerge. (You may wish to journal about what this
   experience was like for you.)

4. Consider the weak and persecuted in our world today.
   Be as specific as you can in identifying them. Ask God
   for the wisdom you need to identify what you can do to
   minister to them as a "messenger of justice" and
   "builder of peace."

5. Imagine yourself acting as a "messenger of justice" and
   "builder of peace" in our contemporary world. Consider
   your own personal ministry. Consider how you need to
   accomplish that ministry. Consider how the world is a
   better place for your ministry.

6. Pray for all those who came to mind. Imagine each
   person and group walking with you on the way to God.
   As you become aware of each person or group, pray,
   "We are on the way to you."

7. As a way of preparing your heart for Christ's coming
   this Advent, decide on an act of service for some
   person or group you have prayed for. As you serve this
   person or group, be aware that you are serving Christ.

Week Two, Day Seven

Enter, let us bow down in worship;
let us kneel before the LORD who made us.
For this is our God, whose people we are,
God's well-tended flock.
Oh, that today you would hear his voice:
Do not harden your hearts as at Meribah,
as on the day of Massah in the desert.
There your ancestors tested me;
they tried me though they had seen my works.

Psalm 95:6-9

As they were going off, Jesus began to speak to the
crowds about John, "What did you go out to the desert
to see? A reed swayed by the wind?...Then why did you
go out? To see a prophet? Yes, I tell you, and more than
a prophet. This is the one about whom it is written:
'Behold, I am sending my messenger ahead of you;
he will prepare your way before you.'
Whoever has ears ought to hear."

Matthew 11:7, 9, 10, 15

Reflections

Was there ever a time when you became clearly aware of God's guidance in your life? If so, what was that awareness like for you? If not, what do you think that would be like for you?

Was there ever a time when you prayed for God's guidance in your life and were mistaken in what you heard? What were the consequences of following that guidance?

What difference would it make in your life to listen to God's guidance and seek God's will first in your life?

What does this Scripture passage and your reflections say about listening to God as a way of preparing your heart for Christ's coming this Advent?

Preparing in Love

1. Begin your prayer time by listening to familiar sounds. How wonderful to hear the gentle breeze, birds singing, a familiar song playing on the radio, the sound of a loved one's voice.

2. Become aware of being in the presence of God as you listen with your heart as well as with your ears. Every sound you hear can be an opportunity for meditating on the divine Presence in all of life. Every person you listen to reveals God's presence to you in a special way and is potentially an encounter with God.

3. Thank God for guiding your life and ask for the wisdom to understand God's will in your life today.

4. Throughout the day, be aware that you are seeking God's will first in everything that happens. Be attentive to the difference that makes in the day's events.

5. Ask for the grace you need to be open to God's continuing guidance in your life. Ask God to forgive you for the times you've failed to listen to God's guidance and did not put him first in your life.

6. Meditate on Psalm 95:7: "Oh, that today you would hear his voice." Listen to how God is preparing your heart for Christ's coming. Reflect on your priorities in life and how you feel about them. Consider changes

7. Do something specific as your effort to give yourself more fully to God this Advent season.

Week Three

Rejoicing
in Christ

Introduction

Advent is a time for rejoicing in the coming of Christ in our lives. God became human to save us, to love us, to give us joy.

In her autobiography, *Before the Living God*, contemporary spiritual writer Ruth Burrows says, "The whole meaning of our existence and the one consuming desire of the heart of God is that we let ourselves be loved." Centuries before, Saint Augustine wisely observed that our hearts are restless until they rest in God. Yet, it is often difficult for us to allow God to love us. We resist: "I'm not worthy." We make excuses: "I'm too busy with my family, my children's education, my job, and all the other major worries of life."

If we could but remember the message of an old but timely carol, "The middle of the night is the beginning of day. The middle of need is the beginning of light," we would rejoice that we have been given so great a Savior, Jesus Christ.

So often we look for joy and fulfillment in people, places, or things that eventually leave us feeling empty and alone. We let the preoccupations of daily life choke our experience of the joy of Christ's coming in our lives.

No matter how busy or stressed we feel, no matter how lonely or empty we may be, Christ waits to embrace us and fill us with joy—just as we are. We do not need to wait until we "have it all together" before Christ will come. We do not need to wait until the house is clean, the job is finished, our relationships improve, the presents are wrapped, the cards are sent. We can experience the joy of Christ's coming here and now in this Advent season. All we have to do is open our hearts and let ourselves be loved by Christ in the midst of the chaos, stress, unresolved issues, and busyness. Today, this minute, Christ wants to give us a joy that no one can take away. Then we, like the prophet Zephaniah, can shout for joy, for the Lord is with us, rejoices over us, and renews us in love every day.

Week Three, Day One

Shout for joy, O daughter Zion!
sing joyfully, O Israel!
Be glad and exult with all your heart,
O daughter Jerusalem!
The LORD has removed the judgment
against you,
he has turned away your enemies;
The King of Israel, the LORD,
is in your midst,
you have no further misfortune to fear.
On that day,
it shall be said to Jerusalem:
Fear not, O Zion, be not discouraged!
The LORD, your God, is in your midst,
a mighty savior;
He will rejoice over you with gladness,
and renew you in his love,
He will sing joyfully because of you,
as one sings at festivals.

Zephaniah 3:14-18

Reflections

Have you rejoiced in God's love for you? In what ways do you experience the joy of God's love in your life?

As you reflect about your life at the present time, what areas cause you anxiety or stress?

What does God wish to do in these areas to free you from anxiety or stress?

How can you help others rejoice in being loved by God?

Rejoicing in Christ

1. Begin this time of prayer by relaxing your mind and body.

2. Today, open yourself to the power of God loving you everywhere, in everything you do. As you drink a glass of water, say "I let the loving presence of God fill me with joy." As you take your first breath of air in the morning, say "I inhale the joyful love of God for me" or "God's boundless love fills me with joy." As you take a shower or bath, say "I immerse myself in the joyful love of God for me," "God's love removes my fears," or "God's love fills me with joy."

3. Today, become aware of how you can be more open to God, who desires to renew you with joyous love. Consider how you can grow in a deeper sense of rejoicing in God's love. Ask God to embrace you this day in joyful love and to renew you with a deeper love for God and for others.

4. Think about three qualities or gifts you possess that God cherishes. Write them down as personal affirmations of your giftedness and reflect on them during the day. Thank God for giving you these gifts.

5. Rejoice in God's presence within you as you share these gifts with others.

6. Think about someone who reflects God's joyful love in a special way. Thank God for the ways this person reflects God's joy to you and to others. Plan to call or write a note to this person. Let the person know how he or she reflects God's joyful presence to you and to others. You may wish to plan an appreciation celebration for this person. A special liturgy, blessing, grace, or spontaneous prayer will enhance this celebration.

7. Whenever you experience anxiety or stress today, recite one of the following prayerful affirmations:

> "Today I will let go of fear
> and trust in God's
> infinite love for me."

> "All stress leaves my body
> as God's joyful love relaxes me."

> "Today I will let God's love
> remove my fears."

> "God rejoices in me and loves
> me as I am today."

Week Three, Day Two

...cheer the fainthearted, support the weak, be patient with all. See that no one returns evil for evil; rather, always seek what is good [both] for each other and for all. Rejoice always. Pray without ceasing. In all circumstances give thanks, for this is the will of God for you in Christ Jesus.

1 Thessalonians 5:14-18

Reflections

In what ways have you encouraged others in their spiritual struggles? How have you reached out to the sick, the lonely, and the depressed during Advent?

How do you live the values of the gospel in your daily life?

How have you shared the joy of Christ with others?

How can you pray without ceasing and give thanks in all circumstances?

Rejoicing in Christ

1. Whatever you are doing, pause and become aware that you can rejoice and give thanks for God's presence in this moment.

2. Look at your surroundings and the people you love. Rejoice in the divine Presence in those relationships and surroundings.

3. Listen to familiar sounds, such as the ringing of the telephone, the sound of a computer, or the whir of an appliance. Give thanks that God is speaking to you this day in these sounds.

4. Open the window and breathe deeply. Rejoice that the breath of God is filling your body, like the air you are breathing, with joy and peace.

5. Touch the hand of a child, spouse, old person, friend, or person in need. Praise God for the gift of touch. When you touch others with reverence and love, you touch God. Let these moments be occasions for encouraging and supporting others who are in need.

6. Make a fresh pot of coffee, splash on a fragrant perfume, or smell the aroma of dinner cooking. Thank God for your favorite scents. Allow them to remind you of God's joyous love for you and all creation.

7. Eat a favorite food or sip a delicious beverage. Let this taste remind you of God's nourishment in everything you eat and drink. Be aware that everything you see, hear, touch, smell, and taste can reflect God's presence in the world. Realize that every moment of life provides opportunities for you to rejoice and give thanks because God is present, loving you and loving through you. Every time you reach out to encourage or support another person, be conscious of how you bring Christ's joy to the world in a special way.

Week Three, Day Three

"My soul proclaims the greatness
of the Lord;
my spirit rejoices in God my savior.
For he has looked upon
his handmaid's lowliness;
behold, from now on
will all ages call me blessed.
[God] has done great things for me,
and holy is his name.
His mercy is from age to age
to those who fear him.
He has shown might with his arm,
dispersed the arrogant of mind and heart.
He has thrown down the rulers
from their thrones
but lifted up the lowly.
The hungry he has filled with good things;
the rich he has sent away empty.
He has helped Israel his servant,
remembering his mercy,
according to his promise to our fathers,
to Abraham and to his descendants forever."

Luke 1:46-55

Reflections

Was there ever a time when you were deeply aware of God's powerful presence in your life? If so, what was that awareness like? If not, what do you think that would be like?

As you reflect on your life today, what are the wondrous deeds God is doing for you?

What are the difficulties facing you today?

How can you experience God's loving presence during difficult times?

Rejoicing in Christ

1. Pray the *Magnificat*, Mary's prayer of thanksgiving and praise, slowly (Luke 1:46-55). Pause after each verse and remember the wondrous deeds God has done in your life.

2. Think about these marvelous deeds. Praise God for each event, circumstance, and relationship that comes to mind.

3. Reflect on how you can do this *now* in the everyday circumstances of your life. Imagine yourself rejoicing in and giving thanks for each important relationship and circumstance of your life. Consider how your life would be different if you lived this scriptural prayer.

4. Use the first line of the *Magnificat* as a mantra, a prayer repeated throughout the day to help you rejoice in God's presence in the ordinary events of life, such as walking, working, driving, exercising, cooking, showering. "My soul proclaims the greatness of the Lord; my spirit rejoices in God my savior" (vv. 46-47).

5. As you pray the *Magnificat*, try to enter into the thoughts and feelings of Mary as she prayed this prayer of praise. (You may wish to record this loving conversation with Mary in your prayer journal.)

6. Write your own magnificat, your own prayer of joyful thanksgiving, for all the marvelous things God has done in your personal life, your relationships, your local Christian community, the Church, or the world.

7. Reflect on the *Magnificat* as a joyous prayer of liberation for the poor, the oppressed, for all victims of discrimination, for women, and for you. Reflect on how Mary's prayer can be a model of Christian prayer for change and growth in Church and society. Imagine yourself acting as if God's Spirit is working in you, in

the Church, and in the world to transform unjust structures and bring about the reign of God. As a result of this reflection, decide on something you can do, even something simple, to bring about God's reign.

Week Three, Day Four

The spirit of the Lord GOD is upon me,
because the LORD has anointed me;
He has sent me to bring glad tidings
to the lowly,
to heal the brokenhearted,
To proclaim liberty to the captives
and release to the prisoners,
To announce a year of favor from the LORD
and a day of vindication by our God,
to comfort all who mourn....

I rejoice heartily in the LORD,
in my God is the joy of my soul;
For he has clothed me
with a robe of salvation,
and wrapped me in a mantle of justice,
Like a bridegroom adorned with a diadem,
like a bride bedecked with her jewels.
As the earth brings forth its plants,
and a garden makes its growth spring up,
So will the Lord GOD make justice and praise
spring up before all the nations.

Isaiah 61:1-2, 10-11

Reflections

What is the most urgent need of your family? your neighborhood? the Church? society?

How can you help?

What does it mean for Christians to serve God by serving the poor and the needy? What would be the sacrifices and rewards for you if you would do this?

What is God calling you to do this Advent season?

Rejoicing in Christ

1. Relax in a quiet place and focus on God's joyful presence within you, loving others through you.

2. Read the passage from Isaiah slowly, as if God is speaking these words personally to you.

3. Be aware of any thoughts, feelings, insights, or images that come to mind.

4. Recall a particular time in your life when God worked through you to help others who were in need, a time when you gave of yourself (time, energy, food, clothing, shelter, companionship), although you may not have been conscious of it at the time. Thank God for working through you on that occasion.

5. Ask God to reveal to you how you can serve the poor and needy this Advent.

6. Pray for openness to know how God wishes to use you: "To bring glad tidings to the lowly," "to heal the brokenhearted," "to proclaim liberty to captives and release to prisoners" (v. 1), "to comfort all who mourn" (v. 2).

7. Spend several minutes in silence listening to God. Be aware of any thoughts, feelings, insights, and images that emerge. Be still and reflect on what God has revealed to you during this time of prayer.

Week Three, Day Five

I praise you, LORD,
for you raised me up
and did not let my enemies
rejoice over me.
O LORD, my God,
I cried out to you and you healed me.
LORD, you brought me up from Sheol;
you kept me
from going down to the pit.
Sing praise to the LORD, you faithful;
give thanks to God's holy name....
You changed my mourning
into dancing;
you took off my sackcloth
and clothed me with gladness.
With my whole being
I sing endless praise to you.
O LORD, my God,
forever will I give you thanks.

Psalm 30:2-5, 12-13

Reflections

What weakness, sinful behavior pattern, or compulsion is keeping you in bondage at the present time?

How is God revealed to you in this situation?

In what ways would you like to experience freedom, healing, and joy in this situation?

What is God calling you to do about this situation?

Rejoicing in Christ

1. Following a period of silence, read Psalm 30:1-5, 12-13.

2. Become aware of any weakness, evil desire, sinful behavior pattern, or compulsion that blocks you from experiencing God's love and keeps you from loving God and other people.

3. As you become aware of this area, confess it humbly and honestly before God. Ask God to free you from any negative or sinful influence that keeps you in bondage.

4. Place yourself in the presence of God. With faith in God's love, ask God to heal you. As you pray, imagine God releasing from within you every thought, image, or behavior that blocks you from loving God and others. Watch God purify your heart from negative attitudes of jealousy, lust, pride, violence, or revenge.

5. Allow God's joy to fill your entire being. Reflect on how God has changed your "mourning into dancing" (v. 12) and clothed you with gladness.

6. Express gratitude for how God has freed and healed you during this time of prayer. As your prayer of thanksgiving, slowly pray Psalm 30.

7. Pray for the grace to be open to God's saving love in your life. (You may wish to record in your prayer journal ways in which you can turn from sin and experience freedom, healing, and joy.)

Week Four
Praying the
O Antiphons

Introduction

The beautiful O Antiphons reflect our longing for the Savior. They joyfully proclaim the coming of Christmas for the people of God. These prayers from our tradition express our expectation and our hope for Christ's coming in our lives.

The O Antiphons, composed by an anonymous cantor in the eighth century, became popular in the Middle Ages. The abbot of the monastery solemnly intoned the singing of these antiphons by the monks.

The Church prays the O Antiphons at the *Magnificat* in the Evening Prayer of the Divine Office and also as the gospel acclamation in the Masses of the Advent season from December seventeenth through December twenty-third.

These prayers of expectant hope, taken from the Hebrew Scriptures, reveal the longing of the Chosen People for deliverance and salvation. Just as the people of God longed for Emmanuel to come to save them, we, too, call upon Christ to come, to save us. These ancient prayers herald the final days of our preparation for Christ's coming. In *Celebrating the Season of Advent*, Brian McGee quotes Benedictine Adrian Nocent's reflections on the profound impact the O Antiphons have on the Church: "These antiphons express the theology of Advent and are the season's brightest jewels."

During the final days of Advent, as we prepare to celebrate Christ's birth, we also prepare for Christ's coming in each of our lives and in our world at a deeper level. Looking forward with great joy to Christ's coming, we pray these great prayers of our tradition: the O Antiphons.

Week Four, December 17

O Wisdom,
O Holy Word of God,
you govern all creation
with your strong yet tender care.
Come and show your people
the way to salvation.

Christian Prayer
The Liturgy of the Hours

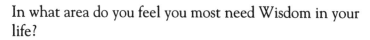

Reflections

In what area do you feel you most need Wisdom in your life?

Where do you see the need for Wisdom in your church? In what areas of the universal Church's life do you feel the most need for Wisdom's "strong yet tender care"?

Where do you see the need for Wisdom in society? In what areas do you see society facing serious issues and needing the guidance of Wisdom?

How can you grow in a deeper understanding of the truth? How can you share these insights with your family? your friends? your local church? society?

Praying the O Antiphons

1. Sit in a comfortable position. Breathe slowly and consciously. Relax your body part by part, from the bottom of your feet to the top of your head. Repeat the word *Wisdom* as you slowly breathe in. Repeat the word *Wisdom* as you slowly breathe out.

2. As you breathe in, imagine Wisdom filling your entire being in a strong and gentle way, teaching you the "way of truth."

3. Become aware of how you feel while you reflect on this image.

4. Consider the new insights you are realizing. (You may want to record these ideas in your prayer journal.)

5. Imagine Wisdom filling the people of God in your local Christian community and the members of the universal Church. Be aware of your thoughts, insights, feelings, and images.

6. Imagine Wisdom filling your family, your friends, and people throughout the world. As you reflect on this image, be aware of your thoughts, images, feelings, and insights.

7. Choose to do something that will help you grow in a deeper understanding of truth. Decide on a way to share the truth Wisdom has taught you with others. Pray that Wisdom will guide and direct you to greater spiritual growth this Advent.

Week Four, December 18

O sacred Lord of ancient Israel,
who showed yourself to Moses
in the burning bush,
who gave him the holy law
on Sinai mountain:
come,
stretch out your mighty hand
to set us free.

Christian Prayer
The Liturgy of the Hours

Reflections

What does God's covenant mean to you? How do you see God saving you, healing your brokenness, transforming your life?

As a result of your reflection on God's covenant of love, what do you feel called to do to live God's saving love in your daily life?

How do you see God saving the world, healing its brokenness, and transforming its life? In what ways does the world as a global community reflect this covenant of love?

As a result of your reflection on God's covenantal love for all humanity, what do you feel called to do?

Praying the O Antiphons

1. Sit in a relaxed position with your eyes closed or focused on a familiar symbol, such as a candle, a cross, a tree, the sky, or a painting. Be aware of your breathing. Gently journey to the center of your being.

2. Read the O Antiphon in a quiet and leisurely manner.

3. Ponder its meaning and contemplate the richness of God's covenantal love revealed in Exodus 6:6: "Therefore, say to the Israelites: I am the LORD. I will free you from the forced labor of the Egyptians and will deliver you from their slavery. I will rescue you by my outstretched arm and with mighty acts of judgment."

4. Allow a word, phrase, or image from the O Antiphon or Scripture verse to touch you.

5. If a word or phrase comes to mind, you may wish to repeat it as a mantra. "O sacred Lord of ancient Israel...stretch out your mighty hand to set us free" can be a powerful reminder of God's saving presence.

6. Become aware of God's covenant of love with you and with all humanity. Become aware of your thoughts, images, feelings, or insights. Be grateful for God's saving work in your life. Ask God to help you be more open to grace.

7. Reflect on what God is calling you to do now as your response to this covenant of love. Consider what you can do to continue God's saving work in your family, neighborhood, city, nation, world. Pray for direction. Listen for God's guidance. Share your thoughts, feelings, and decision(s) with God.

Week Four, December 19

O Flower of Jesse's stem,
you have been raised up
as a sign for all peoples;
kings stand silent in your presence;
the nations bow down in worship
before you.
Come, let nothing keep you
from coming to our aid.

Christian Prayer
The Liturgy of the Hours

Reflections

Can you give some examples of positive changes that have occurred recently in the world?

What possibilities and challenges do these changes bring?

In what ways do you see God involved in these changes?

What can you do to promote social justice in your local area? the nation? the world?

Praying the O Antiphons

1. Take some deep breaths. Close your eyes. Be still and rest in God's presence.

2. Read the O Antiphon in a quiet and leisurely manner.

3. Jesse, the Father of King David, began a royal lineage. Jesus is the Flower of Jesse's stem. The gospel provides the standard by which all nations and governments can be judged. All Christians are called to participate in bringing about the reign of God in the world. Reflect on how the power of God is vibrantly working through dedicated Christians to bring about peace and justice in all areas of life.

4. As different groups, issues, and challenges come to mind, spend some time in intercessory prayer. Pray that God will give each one whatever is needed.

5. Ask God to fill you with the wisdom to see how you can participate in bringing about the reign of God.

6. Pray that God will give you whatever you need to participate in bringing about the reign of God.

7. Today, use this phrase to pray for the needs of the world: "O come to deliver us and do not delay."

Week Four, December 20

O Key of David,
O royal Power of Israel,
controlling at your will
the gate of heaven:
come, break down the prison walls
of death
for those who dwell in darkness
and the shadow of death;
and lead your captive people
into freedom.

Christian Prayer
The Liturgy of the Hours

Reflections

Does your faith strengthen you in the face of death?

How has God helped you through situations in which you experienced grief, loss, separation, or hopelessness?

In what ways do you see God empowering you to meet the challenges of contemporary life?

Do you believe that grace is everywhere and God is constantly embracing you with infinite love in every situation and relationship? If so, what difference does this make in your life?

Praying the O Antiphons

1. Begin your prayer by taking a few deep breaths to relax your body.

2. After a few minutes of quiet relaxation, slowly read this O Antiphon.

3. Recall a time in your life when you experienced grief, loss, separation, hopelessness, or the death of a loved one. As you remember that situation, reflect on how God was present to you at that time.

4. Consider the area(s) of your life today where you most need God's empowerment. Ask God to give the strength you need now.

5. Choose one of these areas. Open yourself to grace. Imagine God embracing you with infinite love in this situation or relationship. Allow the warmth of that love to fill your heart with courage, peace, joy, faith, hope, and with whatever you need to grow spiritually in the situation or relationship.

6. Observe the power of God's love transforming you in this situation or relationship.

7. Pray this O Antiphon throughout the day as a reminder of God's infinite love in your life.

Week Four, December 21

O Radiant Dawn,
splendor of eternal light,
sun of justice:
come, shine on those
who dwell in darkness
and the shadow of death.

Christian Prayer
The Liturgy of the Hours

Reflections

Where do you see the "splendor of eternal light" in your life?

In what ways have you experienced the light of Christ freeing you from the darkness of sin?

Think about a major decision you are in the process of making or will make in the near future. Consider how your faith can enlighten you to make a wise choice.

Consider how the decision you make will impact your relationship with God, others, and self.

Praying the O Antiphons

1. When you are relaxed, calm, and centered in God's loving presence, imagine a beautiful dawn dancing across the sky in bright, golden-red hues, leaping from the darkness of night into the brightness of morning.

2. As you inhale, be conscious of God's light dancing into your heart, filling your entire being. As you exhale, let go of all negativity, anxiety, uncertainty, and doubt.

3. Invite Christ to reveal to you any area where you need to be freed from the darkness of sin. As you become conscious of these areas, surrender each one to Christ. Allow the light of Christ to set you free from the bondage of sin.

4. Focus on the major decision that you are in the process of making or will make in the future. Pray that God will enlighten you to choose rightly.

5. Be aware of any feelings, thoughts, images, or insights that emerge as you consider different choices you could make. (You may want to record these feelings, thoughts, images, or insights in your prayer journal.)

6. Ask God to reveal to you what impact these decisions may have on your relationship with self, others, and God.

7. As you ponder this major decision, pray this O Antiphon for enlightenment.

Week Four, December 22

O King of all the nations,
the only joy of every human heart;
O Keystone of the mighty arch of man,
come and save the creature
you fashioned from the dust.

Christian Prayer
The Liturgy of the Hours

Reflections

Is there some area in your life that you have not yet committed totally to God?

How can you be more open to God?

What is it that God desires to do in your life?

Is there anything you feel called to as result of your reflection?

Praying the O Antiphons

1. In the stillness, become aware of God's loving presence in your life.

2. In your imagination, form a picture of God embracing you. Open yourself to the depths of God's tender love for you.

3. Allow this love to saturate your entire being.

4. Invite God to reveal to you any area in your life that you have not yet committed totally to God.

5. Begin a prayerful dialogue with God about this area. Share your thoughts, feelings, anxieties, joys, anger, or fears with God. Listen to God's response. Realize that this dialogue may go beyond words. You may sense a deep longing for God as you pray.

6. Consider your fears, anxieties, or concerns, and ask God to help you. During your prayer, open your hands and surrender each of these areas or situations to God. Be receptive to all that God wants to do for you.

7. Pray this O Antiphon and open yourself to all that God desires to do for you. Express your commitment to give yourself totally to God.

Week Four, December 23

O Emmanuel,
king and lawgiver,
desire of the nations,
Savior of all people,
come and set us free,
Lord our God.

Christian Prayer
The Liturgy of the Hours

Reflections

How is Emmanuel—God with us—a sign of hope and peace for our contemporary world?

How have you been a sign of hope and peace to others?

In what ways do you see God actively involved in the world today?

In what ways can your efforts show that God is with us? What are you doing to help Emmanuel—God with us—be more present in our world?

Praying the O Antiphons

1. Quiet yourself. You may find it helpful to get into a comfortable position and close your eyes.

2. Be aware of Emmanuel's presence. The God who became flesh, Jesus, is with you now. Open yourself to God's presence in the stillness of your heart.

3. Reflect on any thoughts, feelings, images, or insights that come to mind during this prayer time. (You may wish to record these in your prayer journal.)

4. Be aware that God is present to all people everywhere and that all of us belong to God's family. Imagine the poor, homeless, and destitute people of your area, our nation. Imagine the world waiting and praying for God's reign of justice and peace to happen. Become one with the pain of your sisters and brothers. Allow the presence of Emmanuel—God with us—to fill your heart with divine compassion.

5. Pray the O Antiphon with hope that all humankind will experience justice and peace. As you pray, imagine Emmanuel bringing forth the reign of God.

6. Observe the power of Emmanuel—God with us— acting through you and through others to create a new world order where people live according to the gospel, loving God and one another in sincerity and truth.

7. Give thanks to God for all those who care for the needs of the poor, elderly, and unborn. Give thanks to God for those who help the unemployed, homeless, addicted, abused, and sick members of society. Give thanks for all those who lobby to change unjust laws. Give thanks for people of goodwill who serve the needs of their neighbors every day. Reflect on what you can do to help Emmanuel—God with us—to be more present in our world.

Week Four, December 24

Come, Lord Jesus,
do not delay;
give new courage to your people
who trust in your love.
By your coming,
raise us to the joy
of your kingdom,
where you live and reign
with the Father and the Holy Spirit,
one God, for ever and ever.

Christian Prayer
The Liturgy of the Hours

Reflections

In what ways has this Advent been a special time of preparation for a deeper coming of Christ in your life?

How have you experienced Christ's saving love this Advent?

How have you helped others prepare for Christ's coming during this season?

How have you helped the poor and the needy? What have you done to make the world a more just and caring place?

Praying the O Antiphons

1. Use the phrase "Come, Lord Jesus" as a form of centering prayer to help you prepare your heart for the coming of Christ this Christmas. Begin by reciting it before you get up and before you go to bed.

2. Repeat it throughout the day as you are completing your final preparation for Christmas: decorating the tree, cooking, cleaning, doing errands, wrapping presents.

3. Spend a few moments in quiet reflection. Begin by slowly reciting "Come, Lord Jesus." Imagine Christ holding you close, telling you how deeply you are loved. Relax in the embrace of Christ. Listen as Christ expresses his appreciation for all that you have done this Advent to prepare for his coming.

4. Allow Christ's grateful love for you to fill your heart with joy.

5. Give thanks to Christ for all the ways you have experienced his saving, healing love this Advent season. Express sorrow for the ways you have failed to love God and others this Advent season.

6. Ask Christ to help you continue to prepare your heart for his coming in the midst of your activities on Christmas Eve. Invite Christ to be with you as you engage in each activity or event.

7. As you come to the end of your prayerful reflection, gently return to your activities and/or chores by reciting your centering prayer: "Come, Lord Jesus."

Notes

Notes

Notes